Dealing with Difficult Participants

127 Practical Strategies for Minimizing Resistance and Maximizing Results in Your Presentations

BOB PIKE, CSP and

DAVE ARCH

Illustrations by
Candace Hiatt

JOSSEY-BASS/PFEIFFER
A Wiley Company
www.pfeiffer.com

Creative Training Techniques
Press

Published by

JOSSEY-BASS/PFEIFFER
A Wiley Company
989 Market Street
San Francisco, CA 94103-1741
415.433.1740; Fax 415.433.0499
800.274.4434; Fax 800.569.0443

www.pfeiffer.com

Creative Training Techniques

Press

7620 West 78th Street
Minneapolis, MN 55439
(800) 383–9210
(612) 829–1954; Fax (612)

Visit our website at:
http://www.cttbobpike.com

Jossey-Bass/Pfeiffer is a registered trademark of John Wiley & Sons, Inc.

Wiley also publishes its books in a variety of electronic formats. Some content that appears in print may not be available in electronic books.

ISBN: 0–7879–1116-X

Library of Congress Cataloging-in-Publication Data
    Pike, Robert W.
        Dealing with difficult participants : 127 practical strategies for
    minimizing resistance and maximizing results in your presentations /
    by Robert W. Pike and Dave Arch ; illustrations by Candace Hiatt.
            p.   cm.
        ISBN 0-7879-1116-X
        1. Employees--Training of. I. Arch, Dave. I. Title.
    HF5549.5.T7P46 1997
    658.3´124--dc21   97-21160

Printed in the United States of America

Printing 10 9 8 7 6

We at Jossey-Bass strive to use the most environmentally sensitive paper stocks available to us. Our publications are printed on acid-free recycled stock whenever possible, and our paper always meets or exceeds minimum GPO and EPA requirements.

Contents

Acknowledgments

It takes a lot of people to make a book come together—especially this one.

The CTT Graphics Department, with Sandi managing the process and Candace's awesome drawing ability, made this book come alive.

My coauthor, Dave Arch for his contribution and for the friendship we've developed.

For the thousands of Creative Training Techniques graduates whose questions showed the need for this book. To the current Creative Training Techniques trainers—Lynn, Doug, Michele, Lori, Tim, Rich M., and Rich R.—who, along with Dave and I, collected and field tested these techniques. We know they work!

To each of you and many more I say, "Thank you."

Bob Pike, CSP

Thank you Candace Hiatt for your marvelous artwork.

Dave Arch

About the Authors

ROBERT W. PIKE, CSP

Bob Pike has developed and implemented training programs for business, industry, government and the professions since 1969. As president of Creative Training Techniques International, Inc., and publisher of Creative Training Techniques Press, Bob leads sessions over 150 days per year covering topics of leadership, attitudes, motivation, communication, decision-making, problem-solving, personal and organizational effectiveness, conflict management, team-building, and managerial productivity. More than 60,000 trainers have attended the Creative Training Techniques™ workshop. As a consultant, Bob has worked with such organizations as Pfizer, UpJohn, Caesar Boardwalk Regency, Exhibitor Magazine, Hallmark Cards, and IBM.

Over the years Bob has contributed to magazines like "Training," "The Personal Administrator" and "The Self-Development Journal." He is editor of the "Creative Training Techniques Newsletter" and is author of *The Creative Training Techniques Handbook* and *Improving Managerial Productivity*.

DAVE ARCH, Senior Training Consultant

As a Senior Trainer for Bob Pike's Creative Training Techniques International, Inc., Dave Arch authored all three books in the Tricks for Trainers Resource Library including *Tricks for Trainers, Volume I & II* as well as *First Impressions/Lasting Impressions*. In addition, Dave travels for Creative Training Techniques to over twenty cities in the United States each year presenting the seminar, Techniques and Tricks. For two days he leads trainers through an experience of 119 attention management techniques as found in his books.

Dave has literally pioneered the use of magic in training. Since 1982, magic has proven itself an effective communication tool for groups as diverse as hospital CEOs to sales representatives to banking administrators. Combining a ten-year background in personal and family counseling with a professional expertise in magic, Dave travels from his home in Omaha, Nebraska, to present his unique presentations before some 25,000 people each year in both corporate and conference settings.

Introduction

For more than 25 years, I've asked trainers in many of my seminars
to identify the types of difficult participants they've come across in
their sessions. This request always sets off a spirited discussion, with
the trainers comparing notes, sharing "war stories," and generating a
lengthy list of difficult participants. Few of us will ever encounter
some of the types identified. Some, however, are quite common.
This book outlines fifteen different types identified by my attendees
and observed by me. You'll find a chapter dedicated to each type.
Creative Training Techniques Senior Consultant Dave Arch and I
offer specific suggestions for handling each type. You'll find our suggestions listed in an order derived from the perspective of those who
study behavior management. The first entries are techniques known
as Positive Reinforcers. Studies consistently show that in most situations, people respond better to praise of their positive behaviors than
to punishment of their negative ones. For example, if I wanted you
to develop the habit of putting the cap back on the tube of toothpaste
after using it I'd have more success if I praised you when you put
the cap back on than if I nagged you when you didn't. Part of the
reason for this is the fact that most people don't like being told what
to do, but they do enjoy being praised.

Consequently, at the beginning of every chapter listing, you'll
find strategies that are more indirect (rather than confrontational)
and more preventive (rather than corrective) in nature. Each list then

progresses until you reach, at the end of that list, the strategies that are more direct and corrective. As you proceed through these lists, keep in mind that the strategies at the beginning of the lists are not better or worse than those at the end. Although the strategies escalate in focus and intensity as a given list progresses, you'll find that the strategy required depends on the situation and the personality of the difficult participant.

Some participants, for instance, don't pick up on subtleties. In those situations, you'll need to move more quickly to the strategies at the end of the listings. Other participants are uncomfortable with direct confrontation. With them the more subtle approaches at the beginning of each list are preferred. Knowing whether to start at the beginning, middle, or end of a strategy list will require that you first accurately identify the difficult participant's "type."

Resisting the urge to become defensive, and consequently punitive, will sometimes take all the energy you, as a presenter, can muster. However, jumping to conclusions about a participant's condition (Is she lazy? Is he tired?) will only cause the participant-presenter relationship to become increasingly adversarial.

Changing the participant's behavior should never be your primary focus. Rather, understanding why the participant is acting a particular way is the key to managing that behavior.

In other words, *why* a participant is late is more important than the fact that he or she is late. Likewise, *why* a participant is bored should be of greater concern to you than the fact that he or she is bored. An underlying subtext of this book is that you, as a presenter, can effect a positive outcome with about 95 percent of the difficult participant behaviors you face!

Finally, be sure to take time to study the Application Matrix in the Appendix of this book. From the 100-plus strategies covered in this book, we've taken fifteen of the most common and correlated them with the fifteen types of problematic participants. The matrix provides an excellent overview of the preventive and corrective techniques most applicable to each participant type.

Dave and I would enjoy hearing about your experiences applying these strategies. We can be contacted through Creative Training Techniques website at http://www.cttbobpike.com. Thanks for your interest in seeking to reach all of your participants—even the difficult ones!

Bob Pike

Chapter 1

What (or Who) Is a Difficult Participant?

I've asked the question posed in this chapter title at dozens upon dozens of seminars. Most of the time the responses I get are specific types, like the latecomer, the side-conversationalist, or the know-it-all. Every once in a while, though, the group will dig a little deeper. If the goal of training is to help people acquire knowledge and skills they can apply on the job, then a difficult participant is anyone whose attitude or behavior prevents that person—or others—from meeting the objective. This criteria expands the description

of difficult participants to include shy people and those who are preoccupied.

While it may seem that difficult participants don't want to learn,
can't learn, or are in some way trying to disrupt your presentation,
that's not necessarily the case. Rather, something is *keeping* them, and
frequently others, from learning. In the case of the shy person, it's an
internal roadblock: shyness. For those who are preoccupied, it's an
external roadblock: things outside the class content and objectives.

Our job, then, is to help "difficult" individuals dismantle these
roadblocks so that they, and others, can learn. And this raises the
question: Whose responsibility *is* learning, anyway?

"Who's Got the Monkey?"

Bill Oncken* used the "monkey" metaphor in talking about delegation, but I'm using it here to describe responsibility. Who is responsible for ensuring that learning takes place for any one person? And
who is responsible for minimizing the disruptions that can keep
learning from taking place? Is it the instructor? The disruptive person? Other participants in the learning process? I'd answer "yes" to
all three of these questions.

I believe that the participant's manager, the trainer, the participants as a group, and the individual participant share the responsibility for learning. In the world of workplace learning especially, I

---

*Oncken, W., Jr. (1989). *Managing management time: Who's got the monkey?* Engle-
wood Cliffs, NJ: Prentice-Hall.

believe that a partnership should be developed among all parties to the learning process. And I believe that learning (including training) is a process, not an event. For too long, we've used evaluation forms (in the case of the instructor or the content) and tests (in the case of participants) to judge whether a particular program was successful. Now, I think we must look beyond these tools.

The goal of most workplace training is to produce improved results on the job. Success is measured not in content covered or tests passed but according to what is actually used on the job. If we keep that in mind, we see that responsibility for the learning process—and its on-the-job application—goes beyond the instructor and the participant.

Before Class

The participant's manager plays an important role in determining whether the participant is a motivated or a reluctant learner. Does the manager explain the class objectives so that the participant understands their importance to the job? Does the manager allow time for participant preparation prior to the class? Does the manager help the participant set relevant personal and professional objectives to aim for during the course? Is a plan arranged beforehand for follow up, debriefing, and review of skill application following the course? These are a few of the things managers can do to create an environment that helps participants to develop realistic, positive expectations of the course.

Participants themselves can significantly influence their results before they even attend a course. Success depends on preparation and attitude. Have participants done the necessary prework, if any? Do they ensure that their coworkers are equipped to cover for them so they can focus on the training and not worry about being paged to answer questions? Do they take time to understand the course objectives and how the course content relates to both them and their jobs? These are a few of the things that can improve any participant's class experience—and minimize the issues that tend to spawn difficult participants.

During Class

During training, the two key players in minimizing the effect of difficult participants are the instructor/presenter and the difficult participant. It is to the instructor's benefit to apply the concepts outlined in this book as preventive and positive reinforcers right from the beginning of the class. Doing so will minimize or eliminate many of the difficult participant behaviors. The more participants who buy in to the class objectives and norms—including appropriate instructor and participant behavior—the fewer difficult participants you'll have.

Your Goals as an Instructor/Presenter

An instructor's two goals in dealing with difficult participants should be the following:

1. If possible, to get the difficult participant on board, and
2. To minimize any negative impact the difficult participant might have on others in the class.

Prevention (How to Minimize the Effect of Difficult Participants)

The four main areas you'll want to focus on to minimize the effect of difficult participants are preparation, room setup, group dynamics, and focus on results.

Preparation. When preparing for a class, bear in mind the things that tend to turn otherwise agreeable people into difficult participants: misunderstanding of course objectives, outside time pressures, lack of supervisor support, and so on. Apply the strategies in this book to eliminate as many of these factors as possible before the class meets. Additionally, prepare "buy-in" activities featuring objectives and norms that place at least partial responsibility for class behavior and contribution squarely on the shoulders of individual participants.

Room Setup. In the Appendix we've reproduced several pages from *The Creative Training Techniques Handbook* to emphasize the importance of room arrangement and setup in promoting learner participation and minimizing the instructor's need for control by making the participants responsible for their own behavior. Use this information to design the room setup for your particular purpose.

Group Dynamics. If the participants in your class are like most, they crave the acceptance, acknowledgment, and support of their peers. The more you use small groups in your program, the more this truism will be apparent in reducing the tendency for anyone to be a difficult participant. The Application Matrix shown on page 102 outlines the types of difficult participants group dynamics are likely to help most.

Focus on Results. When participants recognize that what they're learning directly applies to the effective performance of their jobs, resistance to the course and reluctance to participate are minimized. It's critical that participants understand at the beginning of the class (or even before attending) why they were selected for attendance and why the course is important—to them, to their managers, and to the organization. It's equally important that you build time into the program for participants to reflect on what they've learned and to consider practical on-the-job applications. As participants listen to their peers action plans and hear one another echoing the key learning points of the course and discussing on-the-job applications, resistance is further minimized. This is because of Pike's Second Law of Adult Learning: "People don't argue with their own data." By encouraging expression of key points and applications, you help participants see the value of the time they are investing rather than seeing it as time wasted.

Regardless of our best efforts to prevent difficult participants from disrupting our programs, they still might. The following sixteen chapters outline the most common types of difficult participants identified at my seminars over the years as well as practical, how-to strategies for minimizing or eliminating resistance to the course and problematic behaviors.

And remember—it's almost always advisable to use the least obvious technique first. Your foremost goal is to bring difficult participants on board, not to ridicule or embarrass them.

Chapter 2

The Latecomer

This type may be a one-time offender or chronically tardy. Whether this individual's lack of punctuality manifests itself at the beginning of the session or after a break, it holds full potential for disrupting not only your concentration, but the class focus and overall flow of your presentation as well.

1. Arrange the room to minimize distractions.

Whenever possible, ensure that the entrance/exit is at the back of the room (opposite the main presentation area). This way latecomers are less likely to visually disrupt the entire class. If the room has several doors make sure all are locked except the one you want latecomers to use.

2. Start the class on time.

If you are in the habit of starting classes a few minutes late, you are inadvertently rewarding participants who are late and penalizing those who are on time. It doesn't take long for an entire group to get the message and adopt the habit of being late. On the other hand, how do you fill those opening moments so that you avoid having to play catch-up with the latecomers but provide on-time participants something of significant value? (Item 5 in this list outlines some useful ideas.)

3. Always thank the participants for being on time.

Positive reinforcement is a powerful training tool. Instead of complaining when participants are late, try rewarding those who arrive on time with praise and genuine gratitude. We challenge you to try this strategy as an experiment during the first day of class. Thank participants who are on time at the beginning of the class, then again after the morning, lunch, and evening breaks. We believe you'll be amazed at the difference you'll see. Those who are on time will feel valued. Latecomers will realize that this class will start on time. You'll have fewer latecomers after future breaks, etc.

4. Set ground rules.

Don't be afraid to let the group know what's expected. Information has a greater perceived value when it is given more than lip service. Don't be afraid to set limits in your training by setting guidelines that will maximize the learning environment. Better yet, why not have the group help set those ground rules? (See item 18 in this list of strategies.)

5. Use value-added activities.

If you are well prepared, you have divided your content into the categories "Must Know," "Nice to Know," and "Where to Find" prior to the start of training. Now's the time to bring out the interesting, "nice to know" items that won't be covered in the main body of the class. You can use some of these items as value-added activities at the beginning of the class, after key breaks (including lunch), at the beginning of the second day, and so on.

Hot tips and innovative techniques do motivate participants to be back on time. And while you provide valuable, energizing content, you don't need to worry about someone missing the first five minutes and being lost for the rest of the session. As latecomers arrive, they realize that class is under way, and they quickly join a group for activities like crossword puzzles, find-a-words, message-in-circle cards, and group mind-mapping exercises (see the Appendix for samples). These types of participatory activities break preoccupation, are ideal for small groups, and help class members focus (or refocus) on the topic at hand. A well-stocked training tool kit wouldn't be without some!

6. Utilize a trivia question.

Another engaging, yet simple technique is to pose a trivia question to gain attention. Russell Ash compiles a book of such questions annually, separating the questions into lists according to subject matter. (See the Recommended Readings section on page 99.)

7. Give shorter, more frequent breaks.

It's too easy for people to get involved with work-related problems or phone calls when a break is fifteen minutes long. Who came up with the standard fifteen-minute break, anyway? Try breaks of less than ten minutes and announce them more frequently. When Creative Training Techniques senior trainers work in military installations, it's not unusual for the pattern to be one ten-minute break every hour. And it works. Breaks of ten minutes or less allow participants just enough time to use the bathroom, get refreshments, and stretch—but little more.

8. Use curiosity.

Humans are innately curious. Try a simple experiment to prove it. Seal a manila envelope and hang it from the ceiling of your training room. Wait for someone in your group to mention it. Say that you'll open it later, then go on with the training. The power that a sealed envelope contains is amazing! A while later, state that right after lunch (or break), you'll open the envelope. As promised, reveal the envelope's contents—perhaps a folded sheet of flipchart paper inscribed with a content reminder in the form of a slogan or statement and maybe some wrapped pieces of candy for those who return from break on time (see item 9 on this list of strategies).

Here's another example that can help you identify curiosity-piquing components in your own content. Say you've explained to your participants three strategies for accomplishing a task. You might try following up that presentation with a statement like, "Right after lunch, if you remind me, I'll give you a fourth strategy—in fact, my *best* one. If you're three minutes late, you'll miss it." Then, be sure to share that fourth strategy right on time (you can be sure someone will remind you!) and don't repeat it. Other class members may choose to share it with any latecomers, but it won't be heard again from your lips. (Remember, you want to avoid unintentionally rewarding the latecomer.)

9. Offer an incentive.

You state with great expectation, "If you are in your seat at 9:59 (for a session scheduled to start at 10:01), I'll give you three pieces of pasta that can be redeemed for prizes at the end of this seminar." Your choice of token (pasta, buttons, poker chips, playing cards, etc.) is not important. At the end, the one with the most tokens gets to pick from the prize table first!

In some seminars, participants earn points that can be used to qualify for small prizes. Individuals who return from breaks on time can earn points, and entire tables of participants who are on time can earn additional points. Finally, if all participants are back on time, there are even more points for everyone. (Don't miss item 11 in this list; it addresses the power of group accountability.) Usually, we try to keep the rewarding of points on the small-group level. It's important not to change the focus of the seminar to time consciousness or to animosity toward anyone who skews the points. Sometimes, there are legitimate reasons for being late. It's happened to all of us. Therefore, we like to keep point values relatively low to avoid intensifying such normal human experiences.

Lynn Solem, a Creative Training Techniques senior consultant, uses playing cards as rewards. Participants can win cards for participating in various ways, including returning from breaks on time. The more cards you earn, the more likely you'll be to generate a good five-card poker hand by the end of the seminar. The value of your hand determines the order in which you will select from a reward table during and at the end of the seminar. If you've ever been in one of Lynn's sessions, you know how much energy this game generates!

10. Make time visual.

Some people return late from break because the trainer poorly communicated the time parameters. Instead of saying, "Let's take a ten-minute break," next time try saying, "It's 9:47 by my watch. Let's take an 11-minute break and return at 9:58." This causes participants to look at their own watches and gets them physically and visually involved in regulating themselves during the break. Then, as a backup, post the beginning and ending times of the break on a chart or whiteboard. A glance at the front of the room will provide a reminder to anyone who needs one that the break started at 9:47 and ends at 9:58.

11. Build group accountability.

Most Creative Training Technique seminars feature activities that involve groups of five to seven people. Even in large seminars of 1,000-plus, we still divide people into small groups. If you use small groups—and we can't encourage you enough to give them a try— say something like, "I handle breaks a little differently. It's now 9:47 by my watch. If your watch says something else, feel free to change it." (This usually brings a laugh.) "We're going to take an 11-minute break, returning at 9:58. When there are three minutes left in the break, I'll say, 'Group leaders, you have three minutes.' At that time, the new group leaders will have three minutes to round up the other members of their groups and get them back on time. If you're wondering who your group leader is, it's the person in your group who stands up last. Okay, you're on break!"

This interchange inevitably brings more laughter. When there are three minutes left, say, "Group leaders, you have three minutes." People do a wonderful job of rounding up their groups. I like to vary this exercise, making the group leader the one who stands first (this is good prior to the lunch break) or the one who stands second and so on. Since most people will anticipate that the group leader will be last to stand, you'll get laughter in most cases—and a realization that old paradigms don't necessarily operate in this class. This changing routine makes people pay attention, since they don't know how you're going to designate the next batch of group leaders.

12. Avoid making negative assumptions.

Everyone has reasons for being late, most of which have nothing to do with their attitude toward your class. Some may be unavoidable—for example, a sick child or an accident that stopped traffic. Seek to understand before judging a situation. This prevents your relationship with the latecomer from becoming unnecessarily adversarial.

13. Welcome them and express appreciation for their attendance.

The attitude recommended in item 12 will help you greet the late-comer appropriately. The following technique has worked well in our seminars. Stop whatever you're doing and say something like, "Welcome. . . I'm glad you're here. Chris will give you the materials handed out so far, and you can join this group right over here." Your graciousness at this awkward point will make the latecomer grateful for not being put on the spot. If you later discover a valid reason for the person's tardiness, you'll feel especially glad that you didn't embarrass him or her in front of the group.

14. Don't interrupt your training for latecomers.

As you can tell from the suggested action in item 13. we don't want latecomers to disrupt the flow of the class. Avoiding such disruption, however, requires some preplanning on the part of the facilitator. For example, you'll want to make sure that materials are available so that latecomers can get them and be seated with a minimum of fanfare. (You can either offer missed materials at the next break or quickly welcome latecomers and point out where they are to sit.) If it's obvious that there will be latecomers, ask your assistant or a participant to hand out materials to anyone who arrives late and suggest possible seating options. Normally, it's a good idea to scatter latecomers among the various small groups. This provides them with people who can help them catch up and eliminates the need for you to repeat information, which would provide positive reinforcement for a behavior you don't want repeated.

15. Shut the door after the break is over.

We don't advocate locking the door, since this causes too much of a disruption and tends to be punitive in tone. Shutting the door(s) as you get ready to resume instructions not only eliminates potential distractions from the hall but also causes a latecomer's tardiness to be even more noticeable to the group. Experiencing this public entrance just once often is enough to cure a latecomer of tardiness.

16. Make the latecomer the class timekeeper.

For participants who are chronically late, don't be afraid to involve them in the process of keeping time for the class. Have them watch the clock to make sure that breaks start on time. Then, have them continue the job by making sure breaks end on time, too. This, of course, will require them to be back in the room on time, thereby accomplishing two goals with one action.

17. Assign the latecomer a "buddy."

This simple extension of item 11 pairs each participant up with someone else in the class to help them all return from break on time. Naturally, you'll want to pair up latecomers with the more punctual participants.

18. Apply group-generated consequences.

Have fun getting the group to generate consequences for being late.
Then make sure you follow through and assess a penalty for every
latecomer. Creative penalties include requiring the tardy person to
pay a fine, tell a joke, or even sing a song.

19. Talk to the person privately.

As you seek to understand the latecomer, you may find that the person's tardiness has nothing to do with the class or the person's attitude. It simply may be that something else in the individual's life is
taking priority over the class. You can offer to help problem solve or
to reschedule the participant for a time when the problem is no
longer present. You may find, however, that the tardiness does have
something to do with the class or the person's attitude or is merely a
symptom of another problem. For example, the person doesn't think
they need the class or doesn't like the instructor. Or perhaps they
fear the possibility of being called on and know there is a series of
presentations at the beginning of a class. By coming late they seek to
avoid getting up in front of the group. So the person isn't really a
latecomer but rather a shy person. In this case, you'll find appropriate strategies in other chapters of this book.

Chapter 3

The Preoccupied

If you've been a facilitator for more than five minutes, you've seen this type in one form or another. The preoccupied play games on their computers during class, answer e-mail, write letters, pay bills, and, yes, even read the newspaper. Sometimes, their behavior impacts the entire group. At other times, it simply prevents the individual from learning. Whatever the extent of the damage, you'll want to manage the preoccupied.

1. Instruct participants to clear personal spaces.

Ask participants to clear their work spaces of all materials before class starts, explaining that only the materials you distribute will be needed. Participants can place unneeded items on the floor beside them or in personal storage space you provide in the classroom (see item 2). Making this preventive measure a regular habit in your training will take care of many of the physical distractions clamoring for the attention of the preoccupied.

2. Provide personal storage areas.

Designate a place for the storage of participants' personal items. This area should be accessible but not too easy to get to, especially in the case of cell phones and beepers. The next chapter provides suggestions for limiting the disruptiveness of these devices.

3. Assign personal "to do" lists.

At the beginning of class, ask each participant to compile a "to do" list. Encourage participants to list everything they can think of that they must do, especially anything that could cause them to be preoccupied during the class. Then they should put their lists away until after class. This exercise allows participants to "park" their thoughts without fear of forgetting them. Why not even post the lists where participants can see them and add to them if need be. You can even stage a ceremony of sorts at the end of the class, asking participants to get out the lists and take them with them.

4. Utilize more small-group discussion.

Sometimes preoccupied participants serve the same purpose as the warning lights on the dashboard of a car. They let us know something's wrong "under the hood"—for instance, if the facilitator isn't using a wide enough variety of training techniques. It isn't difficult for a participant to become preoccupied when passively listening to a facilitator lecture from the front of the room. On the other hand, it's nearly impossible to be preoccupied when you're sitting with a group of five to seven people engaged in an energetic discussion who are looking to you for input.

5. Give partner projects.

If a participant remains preoccupied even in a small group, try intensifying the technique by assigning the discussions/projects to partners. This usually accomplishes the goal of reengaging the participant.

6. Promote group questioning.

Nothing drains the energy from a presentation faster than the question, "Are there any questions?" Instead, stop the presentation and request that each small group come up with two or three questions its members would like to ask. This technique has a tendency to reinvolve everyone in the class.

7. Review using team competitions.

"Let's review" is another phrase that's sure to cause a classroom's energy level to drop. Try involving the preoccupied in review activities by using friendly team competition. Familiar game show formats like those used on *Jeopardy, Hollywood Squares,* and *Family Feud* make great vehicles for communicating and revisiting a wide variety of topics. Michele Deck, one of Creative Training Techniques senior trainers, has coauthored two volumes on fine-tuning game show formats to involve participants in the learning process. (See the Recommended Readings section on page 99.)

8. Use proximity to communicate.

The next time you encounter a preoccupied participant try continuing your presentation while moving closer to that individual. Then stop behind or beside the person and continue delivering your material. In most instances, the preoccupied person will stop his or her activity, and you will accomplish your goal without missing a beat in your delivery.

9. Initiate a private discussion.

Request a one-on-one discussion with the preoccupied person. Remember that your goal is to better understand him or her. You may find that the participant is overqualified for the class (see Chapter 9) or bored with it (see Chapter 13). Most participants will appreciate both your desire to understand their situation and your discreet approach.

Chapter 4

Cell Phones and Beepers

This chapter addresses devices, not persons, that have the potential to disrupt your presentations. Cell phones and beepers—two tremendous modern conveniences—have proven to be real challenges in many training sessions. Following are six strategies facilitators have found helpful in managing these devices during presentations.

1. Make break times precise.

Participants appreciate this courtesy. At the beginning of the class, say something like, "There will be planned breaks of _____ minutes at _____ a.m. and _____ p.m. The lunch break will be from _____ to _____. Please put your cell phones and beepers away and use them only during the breaks."

2. Establish, communicate, and enforce a training department policy of no cell phones or beepers in class.

Establishing such a policy is only the first step. You then must send a memo to participants and their supervisors alerting them to the policy prior to the class. Finally, don't hesitate to enforce the policy when you see cell phones or beepers in the classroom. See item 6 for an idea on how to store phones and beepers. Remind participants of the policy by hanging a "No Phone" sign in your training room. A graphic of a telephone with the international "no" symbol over it will make the point without unnecessarily alienating or antagonizing participants.

3. Establish, communicate, and enforce a training department policy of no incoming calls during class.

Before the class, send a memo (you could include it with the one you send for the preceding item) to participants and their supervisors requesting that participants receive no incoming calls to cell phones or messages to beepers during class hours.

4. Request that participants switch all beepers and phones to the vibrating mode (rather than the audible mode).

This minimal step at least eliminates the possibility of ringing phones, beeping beepers, and participants checking to see if the sound is coming from their unit. Make this switching of the phones and beepers to the vibrating mode an integral part of the class. It can be presented as something fun rather than something adversarial. Why not make it part of item 1 from Chapter 3, in which participants clear personal items from their work area?

5. Ask participants to reschedule for a future class if they're so busy that they cannot be without their cell phones or pagers at the time of this class.

If the cell phone or beeper is a "must have," remember that in most cases you can request that the participant reschedule for a time when he or she can be without these convenient but disruptive miracles of modern technology.

6. Provide storage envelopes.

Prepare large manila envelopes with participants' names on them. On entering the room, participants can put their pagers and phones in the envelopes. They can then locate them easily during breaks and at lunch.

Chapter 5

The Prisoner

Whenever a class is mandatory, some participants are bound to view themselves as prisoners. They may react passively (with apathy) or aggressively (with anger or hostility). Suggestions for handling passive participants are covered in the next chapter ("The Introvert"). For strategies that address the aggressive participant, or the prisoner, read on.

1. Directly face the prisoner's reservations.

Negative energy is, at least, energy. Here's a technique for tapping into negative energy and channeling it into learning.

At the beginning of the class, ask the participants to brainstorm eighteen reasons they *shouldn't* be there. They can write their reasons on sticky notes and post them on flip charts, or you can solicit several volunteer scribes to list the group's input on flip charts.

When the posting is done, tape each flip-chart sheet in a prominent location on the wall. Then say something like, "With all of these reasons, I can see why you don't want to be here. With all of these reasons, I'm not sure *I* want to be here. But like it or not, you're here and I'm here. I wish I could do something about these issues, but I can't. (If you *can* do something about some of them, state what you can do and when you will do it.) I promise to do my best to make this worth your while. I'd like you to do your best to meet me halfway. Will you do that?" This exercise in venting and rechanneling is often successful in bringing a roomful of prisoners into your corner.

2. Present group-generated benefits.

Seldom does a group consist exclusively of prisoners. Normally, there are a few prisoners, some vacationers (those escaping work), and those who are true explorers—ready to engage with the content. Once these subgroups have identified themselves, take time to let prisoners vent (as in the previous exercise) but also allow the explorers to share why they are excited about the class. This technique has been known to make explorers out of both prisoners and vacationers!

3. Keep all course materials benefit based.

Try opening the class with a David Letterman-inspired "Top Ten List of Benefits for Participants." Make sure all presession publicity addresses the benefits for participants. Check to see if the title and cover of your course workbook address benefits as well. In a market where workers change jobs seven times during their lives, the benefits of a training course need to have applications beyond workers' present jobs. How will the class affect participants' personal and professional futures? Will it make them more marketable? Since these are the kinds of questions participants will ask, the facilitator and course designer must ask them too.

4. Use proximity.

During your delivery, try walking toward someone you perceive as a prisoner and standing near that person. You'll find that almost 90 percent of the time, the participant will look up and become engaged (or reengaged) in the content you're presenting.

5. Enlist their help.

Andrew Carnegie was right on the money when he said that the best way to make a friend is to ask that person for a favor. When you ask a prisoner to help you with a low-risk activity (distributing materials, rearranging tables, posting charts, etc.), you show trust in that person. And that exhibited trust just might be the key to transforming a prisoner into a cooperative, involved participant.

6. Initiate a private discussion.

You might be amazed when you talk one-on-one with a participant you've pegged as a prisoner. If you do so with an attitude of trying to understand, you may find yourself talking to a preoccupied participant, a know-it-all, or even a bored class member. You're then ready to dig into another tool box of strategies for involving this person in your class.

7. Allow them to leave.

Never forget that you do have this option. Just knowing that it exists may relieve some potential panic, giving you the space and time to think creatively about the situation at hand.

Chapter 6

The Introvert

Very little energy emanates from the introverted participant. This may be due to a shyness inherent in the individual's personality,
a fearfulness about the content or the group,
or even suppressed anger that is demon-
strated through passivity. Whatever the reason, you'll want to put some energy-stoking
strategies to work. Introverted participants
can exert more influence on a group than one
might at first imagine.

1. Use small-group projects.

The quiet and shy, as well as those who refrain from participating for other reasons, may respond through a desire to see their small group succeed. An introverted participant who experiences success and acceptance in the smaller group usually is more willing to participate with the larger group.

2. Employ group-generated questioning.

People who are withdrawn are very unlikely to ask questions in front of a large group. To draw them out, periodically ask the small groups to brainstorm one or two questions they'd like to ask. This plants the realization in the mind of all participants that questioning is a normal and expected part of the learning process. Then again, it may be that someone else in the withdrawn participant's small group can answer that person's question within the safety of the small group. If not, the question now becomes one that the small group will pose to the entire class, and the individual retains relative anonymity while having made a contribution to the group.

3. Rotate small-group leadership.

Rotate small-group leadership more often when withdrawn participants are in the training class. Eventually, the withdrawn individuals will have a leadership opportunity and may be comfortable as long as that role is limited to the small group. Our experience shows that the small group also tends to encourage the contribution of its members, including the shy and withdrawn.

4. Ask for written responses.

When an entire training group can be characterized as introverted (like an individual, a training group as a whole can exhibit personality traits), encourage written responses as the first step in getting the members to share their thoughts and ideas. Then, ask some participants to read what they've written to their small groups. Utilizing groups of five to seven people makes introverted participants more comfortable.

One example of such an activity comes from a Creative Training Techniques course. Using a series of open-ended sentences, the "Two Peas in a Pod" exercise asks participants to complete sentences that begin as follows:

1. A person will work hard if. . .
2. People will cooperate with one another if. . .
3. Personal success can be measured by. . .
4. If everybody in the world were the same. . .
5. When I think something needs to said, I. . .

6. My greatest frustration is. . .

7. Others would describe me as. . .

Notice that the first four sentences are written in the third-person voice, while the last three are written in the first person. We start with open-ended sentences that generalize about human behaviors and tendencies and finish by focusing on the person who's writing. This formula could be customized, making open-ended sentences about quality, customer service, or even the applications of various computer software products.

Participants are given about three minutes to complete the written part of the exercise. Small-group leaders are then chosen, and the groups debrief by having their leaders read each phrase, with each group member then reading how he or she completed it. Finally, the entire group makes observations about the similarities and differences among the answers.

This activity helps all group members (especially the introverted) get comfortable with their small group and develop a sense of comfort, acceptance, and safety within the group—which naturally increases the likelihood of participation in the large group. (*Note:* A complete sample of the two work sheets used in this activity can be found in the Appendix.)

5. Use an engaging opener.

Through careful selection, you can use an opener that breaks preoccupation through involvement, facilitates networking, and is relevant to the class material. Within the context of this chapter, the second quality of a good opening (facilitating networking) increases in importance; for when tension is high, retention is low. Taking time to help participants (especially introverted ones) get to know one another as people rather than as just names or roles helps reduce the natural fear and anxiety that hinders retention. Spending a few extra minutes to lower the initial anxiety level of your participants by helping participants to get comfortable with one another is not a waste of time. If you *don't* do this, the content communicated during this anxious period may be missed.

6. Demonstrate the value of volunteering.

Shy people can gain through participating, but may fear being put on the spot. Here's one way to minimize this fear. At the very beginning of your class, demonstrate that with risk goes reward and that it's always a good thing to volunteer. Here's a technique that successfully communicates this notion.

Ask for a volunteer from each small group, indicating that after they've volunteered by standing up, you'll tell them what they've volunteered for. Remind them that with risk goes reward. Once a person is standing at each table, ask each volunteer to gently put his or her hand on the shoulder of the person to his or her left or right. Once they've all done that, say, "Great! Your job is done! You've identified our first small-group leaders!" This comment generally brings laughter.

Then say, "Group leaders, your job is easy. I want you to pick someone in your group, other than the person who got you into this (which generally brings more laughter), to be your assistant." After they've done this, say, "Great! Now, group leaders, your job is to come to the front of the room and pick up enough materials for everyone at your table. Assistant group leaders, your job is to record your group members' answers to this question and post each one on a sticky note on this flip chart."

What people soon realize is that it's safe to volunteer. The class is going to be fun. No one is going to be put on the spot or embarrassed in any way. Finally, they'll discover that the more they volunteer, the more they'll learn!

7. Provide small incentives.

Incentives need not be large or expensive. Candy works great! The idea is to encourage everyone in the class to reward positive performance when they see it. Sometimes we'll put a small sheet of colored coding dots on the table and ask participants to be aware of anyone who contributes to their learning. Everyone should be on the lookout for people who take a risk or take charge of their own learning—who get their own needs met. Participants who observe someone exhibiting such behavior are to take a colored dot and present it to that person by placing it on that person's name tag and are to explain specifically what the person did or said that warranted recognition.

This practice quickly involves all class members, as they become aware of everyone around them who contributes to their learning. They come to realize that it's not just the trainer supplying the instruction. You'll be amazed at the lift people get when they're given a dot—a lift that stems not from the dot's monetary value (less than a penny) but from its symbolism of a positive personal quality recognized by the recipient's peers.

8. Allow participants to participate at their own comfort level.

Whenever possible, try not to violate this axiom. At a seminar in St. Louis, a man introduced himself by saying (in a voice with a very bad stutter) "IIIIIIIIIIIIII'mmmmmmmmmmmmmmmm Elllllllllllll-llmmmmmmmmmmmmmmmmer Poooooooooooooooowell (not his real name). IIIIIIIIIIIIII'mmmmmmmmmmmmmmmm from St. Loui-iiiiiiiiiiiiiiis, Missouri." You could sense that the entire class of more than eighty managers, executives, and salespeople was embarrassed for him, empathic, and concerned.

When we divided into small groups and it became clear that each group leader would be responsible for leading the small-group discussion and then sharing a one-minute summary with the larger group, people became concerned. Some members of Elmer's small group asked me privately if he would be forced to lead. I responded that the choice should be Elmer's. He could lead and report, or he could delegate, but the decision should be his. The next day (it was a three-day program), Elmer gave his group's report, stuttering through much of it. Nevertheless, he did it and the choice was his. On the third and final day, the class participated in an activity involving making choices about how to solve a problem. Then the participants cast their votes by gathering in small groups according to their choice of solution. Once the small groups were assembled, the participants took time to discuss their reasons for being in that group and to select a spokesperson. It was the spokesperson's job to explain the group's reasons for choosing the solution it did to the other groups. During the process, participants were free to change their minds about their choices, leave their initial group, and join a new group. Historically, few people change their minds once they have joined a group. Rather, they tend to look for supporting arguments to reinforce their own conclusion. Most are not very open to what members of other groups might say.

Unfortunately, Elmer's chosen solution had him in a group by himself. You could almost hear the entire group sending mental encouragements to Elmer to join another group so he wouldn't have to defend his position and be embarrassed by his stuttering. When it came time to deliver the presentations, no one had changed groups, and the leaders shared their respective groups' arguments. Finally, Elmer's turn arrived. His presentation lasted ninety seconds, and he stuttered only twice. The entire class gave him a standing ovation, and seven or eight people were so moved that they joined Elmer's group.

At the conclusion of the program, participants had a chance to share their comments with the entire group. Elmer came to the front of the room, took the microphone, and said, "I'm Elmer Powell from St. Louis, Missouri. You might have noticed when we began the class that I stuttered (there was laughter, since we had, of course, noticed). I stuttered because I was afraid of people. You see, I'd been a manager of a fast-food restaurant. The ownership changed, and I didn't get along with the new owner. Thinking that I could do better, I quit. However, I couldn't find another job, so I went back to the restaurant. The owner said he'd filled the store manager position, but I could be the janitor if I wanted. I felt I had no choice, so I became the janitor and was the lowest-ranked employee in the store I had once managed. I became afraid of people. I came to this class determined to do whatever I could to stop being afraid. You might notice that I don't stutter anymore. That's because I'm not afraid anymore. And I'm never going to be afraid again!"

The group gave him another standing ovation, and there wasn't a dry eye in the room. So, by using small groups, reinforcing the positives, allowing participants to participate at their own comfort level, and encouraging them to take risks in a supportive environment, you, too, can help an Elmer (or Ellen) Powell overcome his (or her) fear!

9. Partner selectively.

In activities involving partnering, try to pair the introverted person with someone who is moderately outgoing. The only warning here would be to avoid pairing the introverted person with someone dominant, since the dominant person may not allow the introverted individual to contribute. This experience would only cause the introverted participant to withdraw further.

This technique works well if you have a number of experienced people in the group. By pairing them with less experienced participants, you'll help the less experienced participants overcome their fear of making a mistake, while encouraging learning to take place.

10. Enlist their help.

Encourage the introvert to help with nonverbal physical tasks, such as posting charts on the wall, distributing materials, or checking on the delivery of refreshments for a coffee break. This places the person in a position of responsibility within the class. By tapping into their physical, rather than their verbal capabilities, you gradually draw these people out for better interaction with the group. As you seek to move these participants into more verbal and assertive roles, why not put them in charge of signaling to you when it's a scheduled break time?

11. Solicit one-on-one feedback.

Approach the withdrawn participant during a break and ask for specific feedback on a subject under discussion in the class. If you find the person's contribution thoughtful, follow up by asking if the person would be willing to share his or her insight with the small group or the large group following the break. If the person OKs sharing with the large group, talk to the group about your discussion, then ask the individual to share the insight. You have essentially become a bridge for this participant, facilitating his or her involvement with the entire class.

12. Coach the participant.

This goes beyond the strategy suggested in item 11 in that you visit privately with the introverted individual in an attempt to coach him or her. You should prearrange to call on the person later (during class) and let the person practice answering the question now. By giving them this advance notice and "rehearsal" opportunity, you enable the participant to prepare and thus be more confident about responding appropriately. When the person succeeds, you'll soon find that success does indeed breed success.

Chapter 7

The Elder

This type of participant struggles with self-confidence because of his or her age. Whereas the previous chapter presented suggestions concerning participants whose low self-esteem is a problem, this chapter outlines strategies for coping with participants for whom older age is a factor.

1. Begin with the familiar.

This is always a good tip for trainers, but especially here. When teaching a new skill, begin with concepts that already may be familiar to participants. That way, older participants are more likely to offer input right from the start. Then, build on the familiar by expanding into areas likely to be new to the participants. The next strategy illustrates a specific example of this.

2. Begin with terms and concepts.

Say you are leading a session on the applications of a new bookkeeping software program. Begin with terms and concepts most bookkeepers would know. Then, build on the familiar to show how the new program would enable the participants to better manage those concepts. Terms and concepts can transcend generation gaps; tasks often cannot.

3. Enlist their help.

As you present and explain new information, be on the lookout for opportunities to ask older participants to share their wisdom, knowledge, and experience. Whenever possible, use them as a resource. If they are qualified, ask them to teach parts of the program with you. This involvement can make them more receptive to the new information presented.

4. Share testimonials.

Share a story about a particular learning experience that benefitted someone who was feeling "too old" to learn. In striving to be unique individuals, we may assume that our emotions are very different from those that others experience. Use any anecdote or testimonial that might help older participants feel less awkward or hopeless concerning their fears about learning. A sense of empathy can help alleviate their apprehension.

5. Share historical illustrations.

Remind participants that Grandma Moses did her best painting after the age of 80. Be watchful for other examples to share when needed. There may be people in your area getting college degrees in their 60s, running marathons in their 70s, etc. It is never too late to do something important to you.

6. Initiate a private discussion.

During a one-on-one discussion, seek to understand the older participant's fears and concerns. Ask why the individual feels too old to learn. Identify any obstacles you could help remove.

Chapter 8

The Domineering

These participants can be very clever, sometimes interrupting to share a war story, other times asking meaningless questions just to hear themselves talk. Whatever the technique, they overpower the group and hold it hostage. Getting the group back—without paying the ransom—is the goal of the following strategies.

1. Use small groups.

Don't give the floor to the domineering in front of the whole group. One way to achieve this is by using small groups and getting group ideas, rather than individual ideas. Dividing the class into small groups of five to seven participants can help to contain domineering participants. In the best-case scenario, the small group will exert enough collective power to manage the behavior of the domineering person. Small groups are even more effective, however when you also. . .

2. Rotate group leadership.

With a domineering person in the class, you'll want to rotate small-group leadership often. This prevents the offender from constantly trying to manage his or her group. By using the technique of having the small-group leaders pick their successors, you send another message. Most of the time, domineering individuals aren't selected by the others. This nonverbal cue communicates that controlling behavior is neither appreciated nor valued.

Another way of ensuring that everyone gets a chance to be a leader is to assign a number to each person in the small group and to move sequentially through those numbers as leaders are needed.

3. Use incentives.

Through the use of rewards for participation (e.g., pieces of candy, two pennies for "putting in their two cents' worth"), you encourage everyone to participate and make it difficult for one person to monopolize the class time.

4. Use physical proximity.

When domineering participants are sharing, walk toward them as they speak. Experience shows that very often the closer the trainer gets, the quicker the person finishes talking.

5. Establish group ground rules.

Begin class by drawing a two-column table on your flip chart. At the top of the left-hand column, write the word "Facilitator" (or "Instructor" or "Trainer," as appropriate). Then ask the group, "How many of you have been in a class where the facilitator's behavior ruined the presentation?" (Show of hands.) "Let's list some of these behaviors." As participants voice them, list the behaviors in the left-hand column.

Then label the right-hand column "Participants" and ask, "How many have attended a training session where one or more participants' behaviors ruined the experience? Let's list some of these behaviors in the right-hand column." Again, list the behaviors as they are shared. Post the listing in a prominent location in the room while making the following promise to the class: "I commit to do my utmost to avoid exhibiting the behaviors listed in the left-hand column. All I ask is that you do the same concerning those in the right-hand column."

If you have reason to believe that participant dominance might be an issue, be sure to list it in the right-hand column. If necessary you can later refer to it as one of the "group rules" rather than making it an issue between you and the offending party. If no group or individual mentions it, you might, as the instructor, say, "One thing (or several if there are other issues you'd like addressed) other groups mention is the dominant participant. I'd like to suggest you develop guidelines for this as well."

If the group is larger, have each small group of five or more choose to be either *F*s or *P*s, without explaining what the letters represent. Indicate that half of the groups should represent one letter and the other half the other letter. Once they've made their choices, reveal that *F* stands for facilitator and *P* is for participant. Give the groups three minutes to discuss the worst facilitators they've ever had (the *F* groups) or the worst participants they've ever been in a class with (the *P* groups) and what the offending parties did or said (or failed to do or say) that made them so objectionable.

Solicit two assistants to come to the flip charts at the front of the room. Ask them to post the disruptive behaviors—first from the *F*s, then from the *P*s—as these behaviors are cited by small-group members. Finally, post the flip-chart sheets on the wall and make a contract with the class members that both you and they will try to refrain from these behaviors. This technique can be used with four or more groups and is a good "buy-in" activity, especially for the shy participants.

6. Establish group questioning.

If the domineering individual's technique of choice is the use of questioning to control the group, make sure that the ground rules suggested in the preceding strategy include a group-generated time limit on the question-and-answer period. Then, record any questions not addressed during the allotted time on a piece of flip-chart paper titled "Capture the Question" that is posted on the wall. This way, you control the pace of the class, working in unaddressed questions as the material permits rather than allowing the domineering participant to dictate pacing. As suggested in previous chapters, ask the small groups to generate questions to be covered in the question-and-answer period. Again, this technique assures that domineering individuals are not endlessly given the floor to pose their questions but, like all participants, must have their questions filtered through their own small groups.

7. Rotate groups members.

Despite your best efforts, a small group may be unable to control a dominant participant's behavior. In such a case, try mixing up the groups from time to time. One group might be more successful in managing the person's behavior than another. When rotating the groups, however, try moving the offender closer to you, but over to the side (you don't want him or her sapping your energy by sitting directly in front of you throughout the class). By positioning dominant participants up front, you can better access them when needed (see item 4 of this list).

Creative Training Techniques' senior trainer Doug McCallum suggests this effective strategy. As you prepare to rotate small-group membership, ask participants to each take a colored marker from those on their table (the number of colors corresponds to the number of tables in the room). Pay close attention to the color the domineering participant selects; then designate a table in the front but off to the side as the table for participants with that color of marker. Request that the dominant person lead his or her members up to their table, thereby preventing the person from trading markers to be able to remain in the back of the room.

8. Utilize tokens.

To further equalize participation, try providing everyone with three tokens (fewer if it's a short class). Explain that each token can be used to ask one question or make one comment. Encourage participants to use the tokens wisely, because once they're gone, they're gone. This exercise makes participants think twice before speaking since they'll want to save their tokens for important questions or comments. Consequently, there's less chance that the floor will be monopolized or the discussion sidetracked by one participant.

One additional thought about tokens: If it's a longer class, consider replenishing tokens on a daily basis. At the start of each daily session, give participants enough tokens to bring their total back up to three.

9. Dramatize the holding of the floor.

Make the act of taking the floor a big deal! Use a Koosh® ball to indicate who has the floor. The participant who has the ball has the floor, and anyone who wants the floor first must get the ball from the person currently holding it. You may want to consider using this activity in conjunction with the tokens mentioned in item 8.

10. Physically involve the offender.

By giving the domineering participant an assignment, such as posting group responses on a flip chart, you keep him or her physically occupied, thus preventing interruption and/or domination of the feedback session.

11. Directly question another participant.

When seeking an answer, call on a specific participant—someone other than the dominant person. If that person isn't sure how to answer your question, indicate that he or she can ask another participant for help.

12. Specifically address the offender's small group.

If a participant seems to be dominating a small-group discussion or activity, try this. Approach the group and squat down (bending your knees) so that you're at eye level with group members. While making eye contact with each participant, remind the group that there are X (number of) minutes left. Then look directly at the group leader and say, "Please cover these two points (name them) and try to ensure that everyone in your group provides input on them. Okay?" With this simple approach, you take the floor from the dominator and give it back to the small-group leader. You also reaffirm that input from everyone is desired.

13. Throw a body block.

Use your body to cut off a domineering participant from the rest of the group. Position yourself so that you're standing between the monopolizer and the others in the class. (This can be done right within the general flow of your content delivery.) Such positioning is very effective in diminishing the influence of this type of participant on the class.

14. Exploit their pauses.

As soon as the monopolizer has a vocal pause, look directly at the person, then interrupt with a statement like, "Okay, thank you very much," using direct eye contact. Then break eye contact and direct a question to someone else. By turning your body slightly away from the dominator as you ask the other person for input, you add impact to this strategy. You make it clear to everyone, including the dominator, that you have given the floor to someone else.

15. Build a praise bridge to another.

With this two-fold strategy, you compliment the controller and redirect the class focus. Offer praise—"We appreciate all your responses"—then add, "Now, let's hear from someone else."

16. Make and break eye contact.

This strategy is designed to communicate your disapproval of the domineering participant's behavior in no uncertain terms. As the person raises his or her hand but before the person has a chance to respond, make eye contact and state decisively, "Let's get someone else's feedback on this one." Then break eye contact and select another participant.

17. Deny acknowledgment.

If the domineering person is seeking approval, withhold it until you see a change in behavior (no matter how slight). Acknowledge the person's desire to be heard only after you've observed such a change. You'll thereby reinforce only those behaviors you want to support.

18. Pose a difficult question or assign a difficult task.

As a last resort, try assigning the dominator a task that is hard to handle or asking a question that is tough to answer. Oftentimes, the person will come up short and be put into a more teachable mode.

19. Private discussion.

Be proactive. If you can tell early in the training that someone will be a monopolizer, pull the individual aside and ask for help. Say you've noticed that others aren't participating as much as you'd like and ask for help in drawing them out—getting them to volunteer. If recognition from the instructor is what this individual seeks, he or she will gladly agree to being your secret accomplice in getting others involved.

Chapter 9

The Know-It-All

In attempting to manage this type of difficult participant, it's important to distinguish between the person who pretends to know it all and the one who indeed knows it all—or who at least knows a great deal.

1. Encourage pretesting.

Using a pretest to identify each participant's knowledge and skills in advance can help you separate the "know-it-alls" from those merely acting as if they do.

2. Allow test outs.

If your organization doesn't allow participants to test out of a required course or class, begin campaigning for such a policy now. It can eliminate the training difficulty that comes when participants are made to take a course that they could be capable of teaching.

3. Acknowledge expertise.

Right at the beginning of the class, acknowledge the expertise in the room. A great way to do this is to ask participants to write on their name tags the number of years (or months, weeks, days, or hours) of experience they have. Then have each table figure its total years of experience. By having participants calculate these table totals and by adding them up to get the total years of experience in the whole room, you get a quick overview of what you're working with in terms of the amount of experience in the room.

Lynn Solem, one of our senior training consultants, shares another idea given to her by a Creative Training Techniques participant. The trainer draws a large tree on a flip chart, then turns the chart around so that the picture can no longer be seen by the group.

One by one, class members walk behind the flip chart and place a colored dot on the tree (called "The Knowledge Tree" by the creator of this exercise). The higher up in the branches of the tree each participant places his or her dot, the more knowledge of the class subjects the participant feels he or she has. The lower down the trunk of the tree each participant places the dot, the less knowledge he or she has about the subject. When the tree is turned to face them, the facilitator and the class view an immediate, visual depiction of how the participants feel concerning their mastery of the material to be presented. This knowledge helps the trainer adjust the pacing of the presentation.

4. Enlist their help.

If your organization lacks a test-out policy and you encounter a participant with a vast knowledge of the topics you're covering, obtain as much information and involvement from this participant as possible. Enlist the person's help with report outs, mentoring assignments, quiz/test construction, flip-chart creation, and so on. Build this participant's self-esteem while using his or her knowledge and expertise to help others learn.

5. Consider mentoring.

As alluded to in the previous item, utilize the expertise of the person who knows a lot by making him or her a mentor to others. Ask the individual to coach and explain processes to those who aren't as experienced or quick to catch on. Although this technique works particularly well in computer training situations, it has applications in many other situations as well.

6. Develop challenging exercises.

Make sure your questions and exercises include extremely challenging problems so that even the know-it-all is fully occupied during the activities. One way to accomplish this is to develop seven questions, making one and seven the easiest, two and six a little harder, three and five very difficult, and four nearly impossible. Then

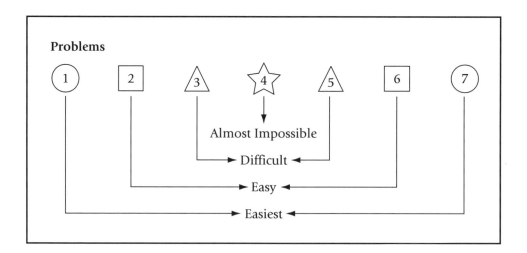

instruct participants to start at number one and work through to number seven or to start at number seven and work through to number one. This process ensures that everyone begins successfully and stays fully occupied and allows those who are slower or more analytical to work at their own pace without fear that the quicker, more knowledgeable people will finish first and feel that the slower people are holding them up.

7. Use an appropriate opening.

One way to alleviate the potential problems of having know-it-alls in the class is to start out by having participants attempt to draw the head and tail of a penny (or the face of their watch, or the keypad of a touch-tone telephone) without looking at the object they're drawing. Then, ask them to compare sketches with others at their table to fill in any missed details. People are always amazed at how little they've seen of something they've looked at so often! This new-found awareness helps make even the most experienced participant more receptive to your instruction.

One of our senior training consultants, Rich Meiss, shares a variation on the preceding exercise: His participants pair up, then turn their backs to each other and attempt to draw the partner's clothes. (Of course, he doesn't issue the exact assignment until after participants' backs are turned.) As with the previous scenario, people are truly amazed by how much they look at and how little they see!

8. Initiate a private discussion.

When all else fails to manage the know-it-all's behavior, ask if the participant would be willing to take questions from the group. Almost without exception, participants who are merely acting like they know it all will back down from this opportunity. (See Chapter 8 on domineering participants for more applicable strategies.)

Chapter 10

The Skeptic

You can see the nay-saying attitude in their eyes before the words ever leave their lips. "This will never work!"—the skeptic's motto—can catch the unprepared presenter off guard.

1. Use intensely practical examples.

Be prepared to offer concrete, real-life examples of how the ideas you're presenting have worked. If you spend too much time talking theory, you'll be an easy target for the skeptic.

2. Present testimonials.

Bring back past participants and have them share how they've applied the course content on the job and what the results have been. This will help prove to any skeptics in the room that real-world results are possible by applying the content you're presenting.

3. Present hard data.

Examine Donald Kirkpatrick's excellent book on evaluating training programs (see the Bibliography in the Appendix of this book) for ideas on evaluation tools appropriate for your organization. Then, you'll be able to supply the skeptic with facts and figures that back up your enthusiasm about the value of the content you're presenting.

4. Make the skeptic address specific doubts.

Don't allow the skeptics to stop at, "This will never work!" Question them on a more technical or process-oriented basis. Challenge them to share the "why's" of their perspective. You may find that their opposition has little or nothing to do with the merit of the class content. Many times, it will turn out to be an emotional issue—for instance, the individual's fear of change.

5. Diffuse their negative energy.

When responding to a skeptic's negative comment, try a statement like, "It may very well not work for you. But I'm going to show you how I've made it work for me and how others have made it work for them, too." Such an approach often prevents a head-on confrontation and can even transform the individual's negative energy, getting him or her to reconsider the merits of the content.

6. Initiate a private discussion.

An excellent approach when talking privately with the skeptic is to use the words *feel, felt,* and *found* to guide your discussion. Begin with a statement such as, "I can understand why you'd feel that way; others have felt that way too." Then proceed to something like, "But they found that the application of these principles did produce the desired results." With these two statements you express empathy

and conviction. This combination is likely to make your next comment more palatable to the skeptic. Follow up with something along
the lines of, "So, the question is not 'Will it work?' Rather it's 'Am I
willing to invest the time to master this (concept/process) so I can
meet or exceed the results of others?'" You will have made your
point in a memorable yet compassionate way.

Chapter 11

The Socializer

If you are proficient at lip reading, you might be able to know what the socializer is saying. It may have something to do with the content; it may not. Whatever the topic, the socializer's side conversation can become a major distraction to both you and your class.

1. Use small groups.

In small groups of five to seven people, side conversations usually
will annoy the others and will be dealt with by the group. It's a well-
known tenet of training that accountability to others increases when
small groups are utilized.

2. Switch to a group activity.

With small groups in place, you can move from a lecture to a small-
group activity if you sense side conversations are becoming a problem. It's difficult to continue a side conversation when your small
group is working on a task that requires your participation.

3. Rotate groups.

If the distracting conversation is continually between the same two
people, rotate the small groups so that these individuals are no
longer in the same group. By instructing participants to number off
according to the number of tables in the room, you ensure that
these two people will end up at different tables as a result of the
rotation.

4. Utilize physical proximity.

While continuing the delivery of your content, physically move toward those conducting the side conversation. Your increasing proximity to the socializers often will be enough to put an end to the conversation.

5. Inquire if there's a question.

Ask the people involved if they need clarification on a particular concept or term. If there is, clarify it. If not, usually your interruption will be enough to stop the conversation.

6. Decrease your voice's volume.

While delivering content, simply lower your voice. This will cause the socializers' conversation to become louder in contrast, frequently causing other participants to ask the talkers to be quiet.

7. Ask a directed question.

Addressing one of the parties by name, ask a question about the material. This approach has proven successful for hundreds of years in classrooms around the world. It'll work for you, too.

8. Pause.

Stop your delivery for a moment and look in the direction of the conversation. If the people talking don't notice, their small-group members will help them get the message. Then simply say "Thank you" and move on.

9. Ask them to share.

Ask the socializers if they have a comment or question about the material that they'd be willing to share with the entire group. By assuming that they are talking about the material, you give them the benefit of the doubt. By asking them to share the comment or question with the group, you let them know you are aware of their conversation.

10. Initiate a private discussion.

Announce a short break and talk to the people involved privately, indicating that you and others are being distracted by their conversations. Often you'll find that the offending parties felt they were being discreet enough not to be heard. These socializers will be amazed and embarrassed that they were being a distraction.

11. Publicly request that they stop.

Ask the socializers in a direct, nonpunitive way to put their conversation on hold until the break.

Chapter 12

The Apple Polisher

The participant really wants your attention. At
first, it's flattering. Then, it gets embarrassing as
the participant's behavior becomes more and
more apparent to the rest of the class. Finally,
it's absolutely annoying—to you and the other
participants. In many instances, this behavior is
just another form of domineering. Consequently, Chapter 8 on the domineering participant will also provide some strategies you'll
find useful in conjunction with those identified
in this chapter.

1. Provide partnering projects.

Have participants work in pairs so that the apple polisher will have to acknowledge another's contributions. This will dilute this individual's inclination to project himself or herself as "the only sincere learner in the room."

2. Specifically call on others.

Deliberately call on others, even when the apple polisher is trying to provide an answer. This will show the offender—and the others—that you respond impartially and fairly to all in spite of ingratiating or solicitous behavior.

3. Employ distance.

While delivering content, move to the opposite side of the room, away from the apple polisher. This movement sends a nonverbal message that the behaviors and comments exhibited are neither necessary nor appreciated.

4. Avoid eye contact.

When addressing the group, stand so that the offending party is to your side or back so you can't make eye contact. This will deny the individual the thing being sought—your constant attention and approval.

5. Delegate an undesirable project.

When assigning projects, don't be afraid to give the apple polisher an undesirable one. This demonstrates to the other class members that you do not reward behaviors like those exhibited by the offender.

6. Initiate a private discussion.

In your one-on-one discussion with the apple polisher, mix appreciation with your admonishment. Indicate that although you appreciate his or her commitment and involvement, you need to maintain impartiality so that everyone in the class is afforded an equal chance to participate.

Chapter 13

The Bored

You've probably seen the look: The eyes are open but glazed over. Many times, however, bored behavior is only a symptom. Perhaps the person is over- or underqualified, tired, or even lacking in confidence. Consequently, other chapters in this book, such as Chapters 6, 9, 15, and 16, can provide a more complete picture of suggested strategies available for handling this type of participant.

1. Change the pace.

Frequently change the pace of the class by using brief "involvement" activities that allow participants to interact with one another in twos, threes, or small groups. Even the bored seek their peers' approval and all but the hard-core bored will participate with other group members.

2. Maintain a benefit-based approach.

Continually sell participants on the personal value of the content. Make sure they see how the content will benefit not only their job performance but other areas of their lives as well. This benefit-based approach should begin with the title of the training program and extend into every aspect of delivery.

3. Remain intensely practical.

Constantly link content to practical application. How will this procedure, theory, or strategy help participants do their jobs faster, better, more easily? Make sure, however, that the class members themselves develop the specific applications (as opposed to your dictating them) so that they feel a sense of ownership of them.

4. Exaggerate the negative.

Exaggerate your bad examples when explaining how *not* to do something. Humor helps lower participants' resistance to learning and focuses them on the content. In one Creative Training Techniques seminar, participants form small groups of five to seven members and spend five minutes designing the worst opening they can imagine for a training session. They then present their worst-case openings to the class. You can be sure no one's bored during those presentations! The results are hilarious, and the exercise sure beats the drone of the instructor reading a list of qualities that comprise a good opening.

5. Emphasize the unusual.

Examine your content for an aspect that's out of the ordinary. If you've taught the material for a long time, you might benefit from someone else's input on which parts are most interesting. Capitalize on those aspects in both your presession publicity and your delivery to help reel in the bored and maintain their interest.

Chapter 14

The Confused

The confused participant just isn't on the same page as you and the other class members. "What was this person expecting?" you might wonder, and that's a very good question.

1. Evaluate your presession publicity.

Carefully read your presession publicity to ensure you're portraying an accurate picture—in both title and description—of the course's content and scope. Too often misunderstanding takes root before a class even starts.

2. Present the agenda.

A good habit to cultivate to prevent later confusion is to start each class by outlining the scope of the course. This helps the confused to know where you are and where you are going. Post the topics on flip-chart sheets on the classroom walls. Then ask participants to generate questions they'd like answered within the topic areas. If they write them on notes, they can post those questions on the appropriate flip-chart sheets. You can also include an "Others" category. While your foremost commitment should be to address the questions in the main categories, explain to participants that you will answer questions in the "Others" category as time allows. This helps align everyone's expectations concerning course content.

3. Brainstorm benefits and losses.

To bring focus to a class—and ensure that everyone is "on the same page"—conduct a benefits/losses brainstorming session regarding the material to be covered. Here's how it works.

Assume you're teaching a course on effective delegation. Ask participants to divide into two teams, the Ps and the Bs. Aim for an equal number of members on each team. (If you're using small groups in your training, each small group should join either the P team or the B team.) Instruct the P team to brainstorm their answers to this question: "What types of problems have you observed when managers don't delegate effectively?" Likewise, instruct the B team to brainstorm responses to this question: "What benefits do you and I gain when we delegate effectively?"

After allowing the teams several minutes to complete their assignments, ask for two volunteers to record the responses on flip-chart sheets at the front of the room. Have each of the P team small groups share a problem, with the volunteer scribe posting the problems until all P team responses have been recorded. Remove these flip-chart sheets from the easel and mount them on the wall. Repeat this process with the B team and its responses concerning benefits. After mounting the "benefits" flip-chart sheets on the wall, emphasize that the focus of this class is on helping all participants learn to avoid the problems and realize the benefits.

Note: If your class members possess little or no previous knowledge of the content being covered, you may need to share problems and benefits observed in your own training and on-the-job experience to get all participants "on the same page."

Chapter 15

The Unqualified

To put it bluntly, unqualified participants aren't up to speed subject matter-wise. They probably should have taken an introductory or lower-level course before enrolling in your class. For whatever reason, they are clearly lost, and their elementary questions have become a source of annoyance and discouragement to their classmates.

1. Define and publicize course prerequisites.

When designing a course, clearly define any prerequisites and/or minimum competencies required for course attendance. After obtaining management approval, be sure to include these prerequisites and competencies in all of your presession publicity.

2. Pretest.

After defining the course prerequisites, design a pretest that all participants must take to ensure that unqualified individuals don't enroll in your class.

3. Assign a mentor.

Occasionally an unqualified person will gain entrance to your class despite a thorough prescreening process. Assuming the individual is not totally out of sync with the content or the other participants, consider asking the most knowledgeable person in class to help the unqualified person over the rough spots.

4. Schedule courses in order of difficulty.

When scheduling your course offerings, make sure you teach the prerequisite course before offering more advanced courses. Your mindfulness of this consideration when scheduling will enable the unqualified individual to take the required prerequisite(s) and the higher-level course(s) in a timely manner.

5. Allow them to leave.

Instead of slowing down and disrupting other participants' learning by keeping the unqualified person in class, allow the individual to return to the workplace. During the next break, contact his or her supervisor to explain.

6. Refer to other classes.

Don't hesitate to recommend prerequisite or introductory classes to participants who aren't qualified for the class you're currently teaching. That information will only help them acquire the skills, knowledge, and abilities needed for attendance in the desired class.

Chapter 16

The Sleeper

This category of difficult participant is most disconcerting for the presenter. Suddenly, a person's head nods forward as the eyes peacefully shut. Little hope for content retention going on here.

1. Utilize group activities.

Physical activity and small-group involvement really help to keep people involved and, consequently, awake.

2. Vary your vocal pattern.

By varying the volume and pitch of your voice, you'll avoid that hypnotizing, Svengali-like tone that can send even the stressed into a sleepy state.

3. Provide ice water.

Have ice water readily available. Providing a beverage without sugar helps keep everyone alert. Although soft drinks do give quick energy, they often have the backlash effect of creating fatigue once the sugar high wears off.

4. Provide coffee.

A hot cup of caffeinated coffee can help participants through a periodic sleepy phase.

5. Plan stretch breaks.

This strategy conjures up an image of the stereotypical presenter who announces, "Let's all stand up now and stretch." But, you can often accomplish the same goal without breaking the flow of your presentation. When a participant completes a given assignment, have the person indicate this by standing up. When all members at the table are done, they can sit back down. This technique allows people to stand at various times during the session without inter-rupting your delivery.

6. Schedule shorter, more frequent breaks.

Don't be afraid to announce shorter, more frequent breaks if several participants appear to be fighting sleep. A seven- or eight-minute break every hour might be just what's needed.

7. Plan physical afternoons.

To stay in tune with participants' natural body clocks, schedule your more cerebral activities for the morning and your more physically active ones for the afternoon. Have mercy on your class members by refraining from scheduling videos (or any activities requiring a dark room) right after lunch. You'll all be glad you did.

8. Have discussion questions ready.

Be prepared to assign discussion questions to the small groups whenever you notice someone about to nod off.

9. Involve the sleeper.

To help stimulate the sleeper, physically involve him or her when there are materials to be distributed or posted on the walls.

10. Initiate a private discussion.

Although it's difficult not to take the sleeper's inattention personally, approach the sleeper privately with the attitude of wanting to understand. It's very possible that the person's drowsiness has nothing to do with the course at all. Perhaps the sleeper is the parent of a newborn baby. Questions such as, "What seems to be the problem?" and "Would you like to reschedule?" should help clarify the issue. You might, however, discover that the participant is overqualified and/or bored. If so, consult chapters 9 and 13 for additional strategies to help the person get involved in the learning process.

Chapter 17

The Substance Abuser

With drug and alcohol abuse becoming an increasingly common problem in our society, we shouldn't be surprised when an inebriated participant ends up in one of our training sessions. However, we don't believe that this is as much a training issue as it is a management issue. The strategies in this chapter reflect this philosophy.

1. Know your organization's policy.

What is your company's official policy concerning drug or alcohol abuse on the job? You need to be aware of this policy and apply it within the training room, when necessary. If your organization is hazy on what to do, you might consider the four strategies that follow.

2. Remove the offending party.

Allow the participant to leave the classroom.

3. Notify their supervisor.

Indicate to the inebriated person's supervisor that the offender has been asked to leave the class and explain your reason for the dismissal.

4. Document the incident.

Put in writing your action of dismissal, including documentation of the behavior that precipitated the participant's dismissal.

5. Refer them.

Although referrals typically are the responsibility of the offender's supervisor, trainers need to be aware of any employee-assistance programs applicable to the situation so they can offer input when appropriate.

6. Initiate a private discussion.

When this discussion occurs in seminar and conference settings, the following two suggestions are recommended:

- Announce a break and speak to the individual one-on-one.
- Ask (or tell) the individual to reschedule and call him or her a cab.

Chapter 18

Concluding Thoughts

The strategies we've shared with you in this book are not merely theoretical slogans. They are practical application-oriented techniques that have worked for us and our clients in a variety of content areas and settings.

One important thing to keep in mind: There are far more participants who want to learn than there are difficult participants. We've focused on the types of difficult ones here to help you diminish their negative effect, not because they are so great in number.

Yet even one difficult participant can adversely impact a group and the learning that takes place.

So keep this book handy. Use it when you prepare for a session so you can minimize the potential for disruption before it has a chance to happen. Use it to refresh yourself on techniques to apply when a certain type of difficult participant appears in your classroom. Use it to bolster your own confidence. Just knowing that you have at your fingertips several methods for handling all types of difficult participants will give you an aura of confidence that likely will make any type of intervention unnecessary.

Recommended Readings

Creative Training Techniques Handbook
> by Robert W. Pike, CSP

In this book, Pike has synthesized many ideas into an easy-to-follow, commonsensical, and, at the same time, insightful set of training tools. Pike dips into philosophy, psychology, and technology to explore the elements of adult learner perception, motivation, and retention. At the same time, he discusses such seemingly simple topics as seating arrangements, flip charts, overheads, magic markers, and so on. As he shuttles back and forth between concept and practice, the creative training process begins to take shape. Pike includes plenty of techniques to keep the process fresh in your mind and ready when you need it.

G.A.M.E.S.: Getting Adults Motivated, Enthusiastic and Satisfied, Volumes I & II
> by Michele Deck and Jeanne Silva

A game is an instructional method: how to learn more, do more, and retain more in less time and have fun doing it. That's the focus of *G.A.M.E.S.*—not a game for the sake of a game, but because it's the best instructional method. Lead your own learning games to increase productivity and enhance teamwork—and get great evaluations and more training registrations! These practical manuals have game directions, time guidelines, application ideas, and even photos of actual examples of game boards and props.

101 Games for Trainers and *101 More Games for Trainers*
> by Bob Pike with Christopher Busse

You'll add spark and energy to your training sessions by using the classroom-tested learning activities, games, and exercises crisply presented in these collections by Bob Pike. Pick from 101 solutions in each book to boost participants' confidence, introduce skills, reinforce concepts, and generate enthusiasm. These games help adults learn without their even knowing it! And they help you reach your training goals and gather glowing evaluations—and have more fun doing it!

Tricks for Trainers, Volumes I & II
        by Dave Arch
Getting and holding attention in your training sessions is a challenge with today's trainees, even for good trainers. Keeping yourself from getting bored when presenting the same old material is a bigger challenge. You'll look great and will enjoy performing these classroom-proven tricks. Dave Arch, the master magician and trainer-of-trainers who pioneered the use of illusions to reinforce learning, has selected these just for trainers. Many can be quickly learned with little practice and use common objects as props. You'll quickly find tricks that fit your content, key message, or learning point. Use these books to wow your audience with your magical lessons!

Evaluating Training Programs
        by Donald L. Kirkpatrick
This book by a former ASTD president outlines the most widely used approach for evaluating training programs—the "Kirkpatrick Model." If management is asking you what they're getting for their training investment, this book will prepare you to answer the tough questions on evaluating reaction, learning, behavior, and results. Plenty of case studies, too!

Top 10 of Everything 1997: The Ultimate Illustrated Book of Lists
        by Russell Ash
A quick source of intriguing facts and trivia on all areas of human achievement and the natural world.

Please call Creative Training Techniques Press (800) 383–9210 to request a catalog describing the above resources in greater detail.

Appendix

Strategy Application Matrix

Across the top of the matrix on page 102, the reader will find the fifteen different types of difficult participants in the order addressed in this book. Down the left-hand side of the matrix, the fifteen most common behavior-management strategies are listed in order from Indirect to Direct, Positive Reinforcers to Negative Reinforcers, and Preventive to Corrective.

		Latecomer	Pre-Occupied	Prisoner	Introvert	Elder	Domineering
Preventive	Incentives	E	G	G	G	G	G
	Involving Opener	G	E	G	G	G	G
	Short/Frequent Breaks	—	G	—	G	—	G
	Ground Rules	E	G	G	—	G	E
	Agenda Presentation	G	G	G	G	G	E
	Practical Applications	E	E	E	E	E	G
	Small Groups	G	E	E	E	E	G
	Group Projects	G	G	G	G	G	G
	Group-Leader Rotation	G	E	G	G	G	E
	Group Rotation	—	G	E	G	G	E
	Group-Generated Questioning	—	G	G	G	G	E
Corrective	Partnering/Mentoring	G	E	G	G	E	G
	Physical Proximity	—	G	G	—	—	G
	Direct Questioning	—	G	G	—	—	G
	Private Discussion	G	G	G	—	—	G

Indirect — Positive Reinforcers | Negative Reinforcers — Direct

G = Good
E = Excellent

	Know-It-All	Skeptic	Socializer	Apple Polisher	Bored	Confused	Unqualified	Sleeper	Substance Abuser
Incentives	—	—	G	G	E	—	—	G	—
Involving Opener	—	G	G	—	G	—	—	E	—
Short/Frequent Breaks	—	—	G	—	G	—	—	—	—
Ground Rules	E	—	E	G	—	G	E	E	E
Agenda Presentation	E	G	G	E	G	E	E	E	—
Practical Applications	E	E	G	—	E	G	G	G	—
Small Groups	E	G	E	E	G	E	E	G	—
Group Projects	E	G	E	E	G	E	E	G	—
Group-Leader Rotation	E	G	E	E	G	G	G	G	—
Group Rotation	E	G	G	E	G	G	G	G	—
Group-Generated Questioning	E	G	E	E	G	G	E	E	—
Partnering/Mentoring	G	G	G	G	G	G	G	G	—
Physical Proximity	G	—	E	—	G	—	—	—	E
Direct Questioning	G	G	G	—	—	—	—	—	—
Private Discussion	E	G	G	G	G	G	G	G	G

Room Setup

Classroom Style (CS)

Chevron (C)

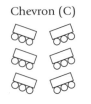

Solid Rectangle (SR)

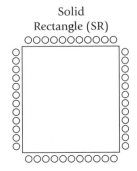

U Shape (U)

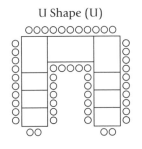

Half Round (HR)

Rectangle (R)

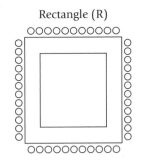

Find-a-Word

```
R  C  R  Z  R  M  Y  L  V  G  N  I  N  E  P  O  F  C
Z  K  P  T  N  V  O  C  E  A  F  Q  P  C  V  S  L  V
V  L  Z  R  O  W  X  T  N  A  R  C  X  Y  N  X  I  I
M  R  F  A  I  G  D  K  I  E  R  I  V  J  E  Z  P  S
A  K  U  I  T  K  N  D  L  V  R  N  E  V  X  P  C  U
R  X  N  N  A  M  J  I  X  Y  A  A  I  T  P  K  H  A
K  S  B  E  R  A  V  R  N  V  T  T  P  N  Y  X  A  L
E  Y  Z  R  A  A  F  T  H  I  A  B  I  S  G  N  R  S
R  D  P  S  P  Y  S  I  Z  E  A  X  J  O  N  Q  T  K
S  V  J  N  E  I  U  U  R  W  V  R  B  Z  N  A  P  V
J  A  Q  S  R  K  I  C  R  V  J  O  T  V  W  Z  R  U
A  U  U  V  P  C  L  O  S  I  N  G  X  P  M  W  V  T
```

CLOSING	MARKERS	TRAINING
CREATIVE	MOTIVATION	TRANSPARENCY
FLIPCHART	OPENING	VARIETY
FUN	PREPARATION	VISUALS
LEARNING	TRAINERS	

Solution

Column #

Line #	1	2	3	4	5	6	7	8	9	10	11	12	13	14	15	16	17	18	
1	-	-	-	-	-	M	Y	L	V	G	N	I	N	E	P	O	F	-	1
2	-	-	-	T	N	-	O	C	E	-	-	-	-	-	-	-	L	V	2
3	-	-	-	R	O	-	-	T	N	A	R	-	-	-	-	-	I	I	3
4	M	-	F	A	I	G	-	-	I	E	R	I	-	-	E	-	P	S	4
5	A	-	U	I	T	-	N	-	-	V	R	N	E	V	-	-	C	U	5
6	R	-	N	N	A	-	-	I	-	-	A	A	I	T	-	-	H	A	6
7	K	-	-	E	R	-	-	-	N	-	-	T	P	N	Y	-	A	L	7
8	E	-	-	R	A	-	-	-	-	I	A	-	I	S	G	-	R	S	8
9	R	-	-	S	P	-	-	-	-	E	A	-	-	O	N	-	T	-	9
10	S	-	-	-	E	-	-	R	-	-	R	-	-	N	A	-	-	-	10
11	-	-	-	-	R	-	-	C	-	-	-	-	T	-	-	-	R	-	11
12	-	-	-	-	P	C	L	O	S	I	N	G	-	-	-	-	-	T	12
	2		4		6		8		10		12		14		16		18		

Words are found starting in row R,
column C, going in direction D

Word	R	C	D
CLOSING	12	6	E
CREATIVE	11	8	NE
FLIPCHART	1	17	S
FUN	4	3	S
LEARNING	1	8	SE
MARKERS	4	1	S
MOTIVATION	1	6	SE
OPENING	1	16	W
PREPARATION	12	5	N
TRAINERS	2	4	S
TRAINING	11	13	NW
TRANSPARENCY	12	18	NW
VARIETY	1	9	SE
VISUALS	2	18	S

Crossword Puzzle

ACROSS CLUES

2. Minimize this by holding programs off-site.
7. Give frequent stretch breaks, but they must be_ _ _ _ _ _ _ _ _.
8. A good brochure turns program outlines into program _ _ _ _ _ _ _ _.
10. Clear questions can help you get answers that are _ _ _ _ _.
11. A precise set of instructions for solving a problem.
13. Besides focusing on content you want to focus on your _ _ _ _ _ _ _ _.
15. Dressing a little better than is expected shows your audience _ _ _ _ _ _ _.
16. Having an agreed upon master performer is one of two _ _ _ _ _ _ _ _ _ _ for using observation for analysis.
17. When participants ask questions _ _ _ _ _ _.

DOWN CLUES

1. Promising _ _ _ _ _ _ _ _ will help people give thorough, thoughtful complete evaluations.
3. A good program announcement has a strong _ _ _ _ _.
4. Visual aids provide this for a presentation.
5. One way of promoting networking is to use an _ _ _ _ _ _ _ _ _ _.
6. One of the greatest needs of any human being.
9. Make sure the topics are useful and that each gets the right amount of _ _ _ _.
11. Maximize the benefit of an outside speaker by making time _ _ _ _ _ _ _ _ before and after.
12. Good evaluation questions stimulate participant _ _ _ _ _ _ _ _ _ _ _.
14. Lack of eye contact can be caused by being _ _ _ _ _ _ _ _ _.

Solution

Across and down solution words:

- interruption
- controlled
- benefits
- clear
- algorithm
- audience
- respect
- conditions
- listen
- feedback
- support
- icebreaker
- time
- available
- involvement
- appreciation
- title
- notebound

Word List

Algorithm	Controlled	Listen	Appreciation	Conditions	Notebound
Audience	Feedback	Respect	Available	Icebreaker	Support
Benefits	Interruptions	Title	Clear	Involvement	Time

Message-in-Circle Card

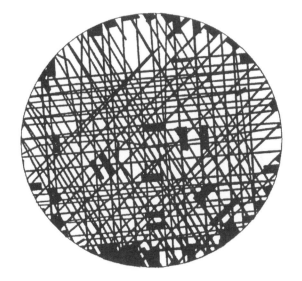

Look across the circle. What does it say?

Solution

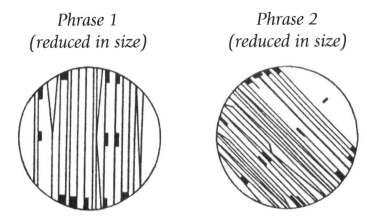

Phrase 1
(reduced in size)

Phrase 2
(reduced in size)

The key to solving the puzzle is to hold the circle at eye level, perpendicular to your body. The first phrase you should be able to read is, "If you like fun"; rotate the circle clockwise 15 degrees and line up the next set of elongated straight lines; you'll see the second phrase, "and learning too"; rotate the circle 90 degrees from the starting point; you'll see the third phrase, "Creative Training"; another 15-degree turn brings you to the final phrase, "is for you."

Making Your Own

Follow this five-step process to develop your own card. Outside the circle include a key message from your training that will be a reminder to trainees each time they share this icebreaker.

1. Select you own phrase.
2. Draw a circle on paper.
3. Using long, thin lines that extend fully across the circle, draw your first phrase. Use bars for extensions of letters like E and F. See the samples below.
4. Draw the second phrase on a separate sheet. Using a copy machine, lay this second sheet (rotated about 15 degrees counterclockwise) over the sheet with the first phrase.
5. Rotate the page approximately 90 degrees counterclockwise from your starting point as you add the third phrase. Rotate the page another 15 degrees counterclockwise to overlay a fourth (maximum) phrase.

Mind Mapping

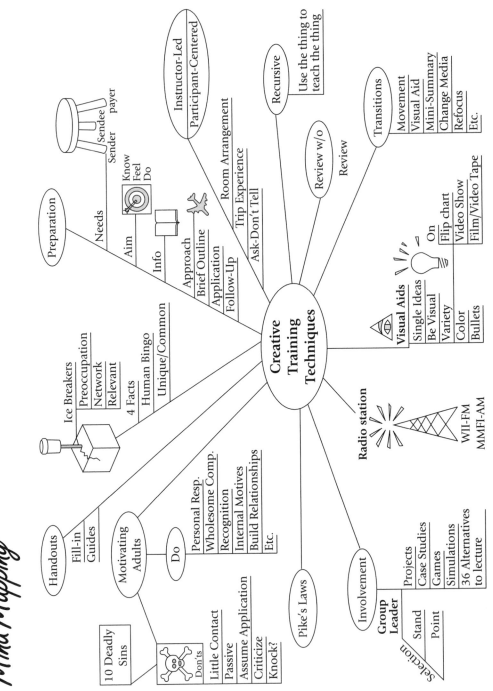

Creative Training Techniques

Preparation
- Needs
- Aim — Know / Feel / Do
- Info
- Sender / Sendee — Sender / payer

Approach
- Brief Outline
- Application
- Follow-Up

Instructor-Led / Participant-Centered

Room Arrangement
- Trip Experience
- Ask-Don't Tell

Recursive
- Use the thing to teach the thing

Review w/o — Review

Transitions
- Movement
- Visual Aid
- Mini-Summary
- Change Media
- Refocus
- Etc.

Visual Aids
- Single Ideas
- Be Visual
- Variety
- Color
- Bullets
- On — Flip chart / Video Show / Film/Video Tape

Radio station
- WII-FM
- MMFI-AM

Involvement
- Projects
- Case Studies
- Games
- Simulations
- 36 Alternatives to lecture

Group Leader
- Stand
- Point
- Selection

Pike's Laws

Motivating Adults
- Do
  - Personal Resp.
  - Wholesome Comp.
  - Recognition
  - Internal Motives
  - Build Relationships
  - Etc.
- Don'ts
  - Little Contact
  - Passive
  - Assume Application
  - Criticize
  - Knock?

10 Deadly Sins

Handouts
- Fill-in
- Guides

Ice Breakers
- Preoccupation
- Network
- Relevant
- 4 Facts
- Human Bingo
- Unique/Common

Two Peas in a Pod

For the next three minutes, please complete the phrases listed below by filling in the blanks. Please try to give an immediate response. Since you will be discussing your responses in your next project, please do not share your answers until that project has been distributed.

1. A person will work hard if... _____

   _____

2. People will cooperate with one another if... _____

   _____

3. Personal success can be measured by... _____

   _____

4. If everybody in the world was the same... _____

   _____

5. When I think something needs to be said I... _____

   _____

6. My greatest frustration is... _____

   _____

7. Others would describe me as... _____

   _____

Verrrrrrrry Interesting

The group leader should read the following: "In 'Two Peas in a Pod' you had an opportunity to respond to a number of sentence stems. Let's take a look at the way we completed them. I'll read the beginning part of the first phrase and then, starting with the person on my left, we'll each share how we completed the statement. I'll share how I completed mine last and then I'll read the second phrase. We'll have a chance to discuss how we completed them after we've shared our answers to all seven."

After the group members have finished sharing their responses, please read aloud and discuss the questions below.

1. Some of the answers given may have been similar. How could you explain this?
2. Which of the phrases generated some very different answers? How could these different ways of answering be explained?
3. Was there any right or wrong way of completing any of these phrases? Why?
4. What were your thoughts and feelings when someone completed a phrase in a different way than you did?
5. What benefits are there in working with and interacting with people who are different from you? What would it be like to work with people who were all just exactly like you—with the same methods, attitudes, and feelings that you have?

WIN *Rave Reviews*
on your next **Presentation**

"I have never felt so enthusiastic about a program! This workshop is a MUST for any trainer, regardless of level of experience."

Susan Russell, Bank One

Do you talk so people really listen?

Bob Pike's Creative Training Techniques™ Seminar

Find out why over 65,000 trainers love Creative Training Techniques. What makes this seminar so different? You'll learn how to get your participants enthusiastically involved in the training. By creating an interactive learning environment, you'll watch the attendees excitement go up and up and up. The result? Your group will easily learn twice as much. When they apply their new skills on the job, you'll see dramatic results.

Learn a revolutionary training approach—Participant-Centered Training. This teaching style is far more effective than traditional lecture-based training. Over 65,000 trainers world-wide have attended this seminar and applied these participant-centered training techniques to their work environments. More effective training means a more valuable and effective work force. Register today so you can get rave reviews on your next presentation. Over 140 public seminars are scheduled in 40 different cities each year.

In-house Training Seminars

Customized programs for trainers, sales staff, and technical presenters developed for 100s of organizations. Give us a call so we can discuss how to help your company increase work force performance by maximizing the impact of your training. Just a few of our clients who have brought Creative Training Techniques programs in-house:

American Express • AT&T • GE Plastics • State Farm Insurance • 3M • Tonka Corporation

Creative Solutions Catalog
Insider's Tips to Double the Impact of Your Presentation

Filled with fun, stimulating, creative resources including games, magic, music, wuzzles, books, tapes, videos, software, presentation graphics—everything you need to make your presentation an absolute winner.

Bob Pike's
Creative Training Techniques™ Train-the-Trainer Conference

The only conference dedicated exclusively to the participant-centered approach to training

- Learn about the revolutionary, participant-centered training approach—the breakthrough alternative to lecture-based training
- See the nation's leading training consultants model their very best participant-centered activities
- Experience the power of participant-centered techniques to dramatically increase retention
- Learn about innovative training transfer techniques adopted by leading Fortune 500 companies
- Discover powerful management strategies that clearly demonstrate the business results for your training programs

Just a few of the companies who have sent groups (not just individuals) to the Conference

**American Express • AT&T • Caterpillar • First Bank
Southern Nuclear Operating Company • State Farm • United HealthCare • US West**

Rave Reviews!

"I refer to my conference workbook all the time. I've shared the techniques with my trainers, and my own evaluations have improved. Our needs analysis now produces actionable input. My comfort level with our line managers has increased—at my first meeting with them where I used what I learned at the conference, they applauded. Now that's positive feedback!"
Gretchen Gospodarek, Training Manager, **TCF Bank Wisconsin**

"For any trainer who wants to move beyond lecture-based training, I recommend Bob Pike's participant-centered seminars and in-house consultants."
Ken Blanchard, Co-Author of *The One-Minute Manager*

"Bob Pike is creating a new standard in the industry by which all other programs will soon be measured."
Elliott Masie, President, **The MASIE Center**

Visit our Web site: www.cttbobpike.com to learn more about the Conference, Creative Training Techniques International, Inc. or the Participant-Centered Training approach.

1–800–383–9210
www.cttbobpike.com

Creative Training Techniques International, Inc. • 7620 W. 78th St., Mpls., MN 55439 • 612-829-1954 • Fax 612-829-0260

13 Questions to Ask *Before* You Bring Anyone In-House

An in-house program is an investment. You want to ensure high return. Here are 13 questions to ask before you ask anyone to train your trainers (or train anyone else!).

1. What kind of measurable results have other clients had from your training?
2. How much experience does this company have in training trainers?
3. Is this 100 percent of what the company does or just part of what it does?
4. How experienced are the trainers who will work with our people?
5. How experienced are your trainers in maximizing training transfer to the job?
6. Is the program tailored to my needs, or is it the same content as the public program?
7. Why is an in-house program to our advantage?
8. Is team-building a by-product of the seminar?
9. Is there immediate application of new skills during the training session?
10. What kinds of resource and reference materials do we get?
11. What type of pre-course preparation or post-course follow-up do you do?
12. How are our participants recognized for their achievements?
13. Will you teach my trainers how to get participant buy-in, even from the difficult participant?

Advantages of a Customized, In-House Program with Creative Training Techniques™ International, Inc.

Customized in-house programs provide your organization with training tailored to your specific needs. Our unique participant-centered teaching style is a revolutionary new training approach that is far more effective than traditional lecture-based training. This training approach has been adapted by a wide range of industries including healthcare, finance, communications, government, and non-profit agencies. Our clients include American Express, AT&T, Hewlett-Packard, 3M, U.S. Healthcare, and Tonka Corporation. We are eager to learn about your training needs and discuss how we can provide solutions. Please give us a call so we can help your company create a more vital and effective workforce.

Creative Training Techniques International, Inc.

1–800–383–9210
www.cttbobpike.com

Creative Training Techniques International, Inc. • 7620 W. 78th St., Mpls., MN 55439 • 612-829-1954 • Fax 612-829-0260

More Great Resources from Pfeiffer!

50 Creative Training Closers
Innovative Ways to End Your Training with IMPACT!

Lynn Solem, Bob Pike, CSP, CPAE

Go out with a BANG!

They'll forget you as soon as you walk out the door . . . unless you make your training memorable. This essential resource is your way to make your mark. These 50 sure-fire training session closers dramatically improve retentiveness because they leave participants with an unforgettable, memory-jogging impression. Training experts Solem and Pike list the necessary time and equipment for each closer, along with a suggested group size, and an intended purpose, so you can choose the one that best serves your presentation. You'll have no problem finding a closer that's just right for your needs.

You'll get activities great for:

- **Making** action plans
- **Reviewing** material
- **Celebrating** success
- **Motivating** participants. . . and more!

With this book as your resource, you will get all the essentials, making preparation quick, easy, and exciting. This book is training dynamite: make it your secret weapon today!

. . . .

50 Creative Training Closers / 136 pages / paperback

Getting Together
Icebreakers and Group Energizers

Lorraine L. Ukens

These brief, interactive games and activities raise your participants' awareness and prepare them to learn something new. Designed to be fun and energizing, the activities help people overcome the initial anxiety common among new acquaintances or in group situations.

Use these games to:

- **Promote** interaction
- **Introduce** your topic
- **Ease** anxieties regarding sensitive or emotional issues
- **Form** partnerships or teams during the session
- **Help** people feel comfortable with the environment, the topic to be discussed, and one another
- **Gain** control of a group
- **Get** meetings started on a stimulating note

This collection is conveniently divided into two categories: 1) icebreakers, which encourage "mixing"; and 2) group challenges, which energize and build team cohesion.

Each game is presented in a concise and easy-to-follow format. You'll get details on objectives, material requirements, preparation, activity instructions, variations, discussion questions, group size, time requirements, and reproducible worksheets or material templates.

Use these icebreakers today to energize your group for the work ahead!

. . . .

Getting Together / 224 pages / paperback

 TO ORDER, CALL FREE: 800-274-4434   **OR FAX FREE: 800-569-0443**